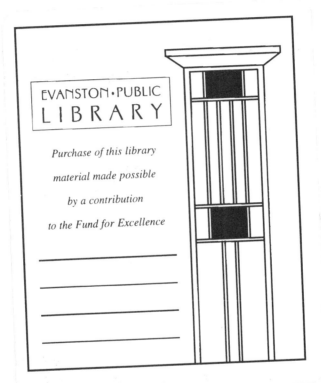

WAR PLANES

Tactical Fighters:
The F-15 Eagles
by Michael and Gladys Green

CAPSTONE
HIGH-INTEREST
BOOKS

an imprint of Capstone Press
Mankato, Minnesota

Capstone High-Interest Books are published by Capstone Press
151 Good Counsel Drive, P.O. Box 669, Mankato, Minnesota 56002
http://www.capstone-press.com

Library of Congress Cataloging-in-Publication Data
Green, Michael, 1952–
    Tactical fighters: the F-15 Eagles/by Michael and Gladys Green.
    p. cm.—(War planes)
    Summary: Introduces the F-15 Eagles, their specifications, weapons, missions, and
future in the Air Force.
    Includes bibliographical references and index.
    ISBN 0-7368-1511-2 (hardcover)
    1. Eagle (Jet fighter plane)—Juvenile literature. [1. Eagle (Jet fighter plane)
2. Fighter planes.] I. Green, Gladys, 1954– II. Title. III. Series.
UG1242.F5 G715 2003
623.7'464—dc21   2002007928

Editorial Credits
Carrie Braulick, editor; Eric Kudalis, product planning editor; Timothy Halldin,
    series designer; Gene Bentdahl and Molly Nei, book designers; Jo Miller,
    photo researcher

Photo Credits
Boeing Management Company, 13
Defense Visual Information Center, 1, 4, 7, 9, 16–17, 18, 20, 23, 26, 29
Photo by Ted Carlson/Fotodynamics, 10, 24
Photri-Microstock, cover

**Special thanks to Michelle M. Weiss, Air Combat Command Public Affairs
Office, for her assistance in preparing this book.**

1 2 3 4 5 6 08 07 06 05 04 03

Table of Contents

Chapter One

Learn About

- The F-15's mission
- F-15 design
- F-15 models

The F-15 in Action

Late one night, four U.S. Air Force pilots fly F-15 Eagle fighter planes over a friendly country. A radio message tells them 10 enemy planes are approaching.

The F-15 pilots turn their aircraft toward the enemy planes. A powerful radar in each F-15's nose locates the other planes about 100 miles (160 kilometers) away. The enemy pilots fire missiles at the F-15s. The F-15 pilots turn sharply and dive at high speeds to avoid the missiles. They then fire their own missiles at the enemy planes. Four of the enemy fighters explode.

The F-15 pilots fire more missiles. Another four enemy planes explode. The last two enemy pilots turn around and try to fly away. The F-15 pilots catch up to them and use their machine guns to shoot the planes down.

Building the F-15

In the early 1960s, the Air Force wanted fast planes that could easily defeat enemy planes. During the late 1940s, the Air Force had used F-86 Sabres for this purpose. The Air Force wanted to replace F-86 Sabres with improved fighters.

In 1972, aircraft manufacturer McDonnell Douglas produced a test model of a one-seat fighter called the F-15A. In 1974, the Air Force began to fly final models of the F-15A and F-15B. The F-15B is a two-seat training version of the F-15A.

McDonnell Douglas continued to produce other F-15 models for the Air Force. In 1979, the improved F-15C one-seat model entered Air Force service. Later that year, Air Force pilots began to fly a two-seat training version of the F-15C called the F-15D.

The F-15E is designed to attack ground targets.

The F-15E Strike Eagle is the newest F-15 model. It entered Air Force service in 1988. Today, the Air Force flies more than 200 F-15Es. The two-seat F-15E has a different mission from other F-15s. It is designed mainly to attack ground targets.

The Boeing Company bought the McDonnell Douglas Corporation in 1997. Boeing then continued to build F-15Es for the Air Force.

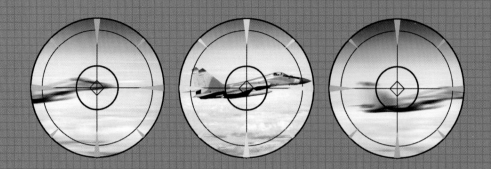

About the F-15

The F-15 is one of the world's most advanced fighter planes. It has a perfect combat record. No enemy forces have shot down an F-15 during combat.

Today, the Air Force has more than 720 F-15s. Air Force pilots fly the F-15C, the F-15D, and the F-15E Strike Eagle. Air National Guard units use the F-15A and the F-15B to support the Air Force.

The U.S. Air Force is the only air force that uses the F-15E. The air forces of Israel, Saudi Arabia, and Japan fly other F-15 models.

The Air Force has more than 700 F-15s in service.

Chapter Two

Learn About

- F-15 engines
- F-15 controls
- LANTIRN system

Inside the F-15

The F-15 is a large aircraft compared to other modern fighters. It is more than 63 feet (19 meters) long. The distance between its wings is almost 43 feet (13 meters). This large wingspan helps the plane quickly rise into the air. The F-15 is almost 19 feet (6 meters) tall.

The F-15's size gives its pilots advantages. The F-15 flies farther and faster than smaller fighters. It also carries more weapons than smaller fighters.

Powerful Engines

Two large jet engines power each F-15. Each F-15C and F-15D engine produces almost 23,450 pounds (10,637 kilograms) of thrust to push the aircraft through the air. Each F-15E engine produces 29,000 pounds (13,154 kilograms) of thrust. Jet engines burn fuel to produce thrust. Hot gases called exhaust leave the jet engines at the plane's rear. The plane moves forward as the exhaust rushes out of the engines.

The F-15 is the fastest fighter in the world. Its engines give it a top speed of 1,875 miles (3,017 kilometers) per hour. But pilots usually fly the F-15 at high speeds only when flying into or out of battle areas. Fighter pilots often need to turn sharply. A fighter flying at top speed cannot turn without slowing down. F-15 pilots usually fly at speeds of less than 600 miles (966 kilometers) per hour.

Inside the Cockpit

The pilot sits in a cockpit in the front of the plane. A clear plastic dome called a canopy surrounds the pilot. It allows the pilot to clearly see the plane's surroundings.

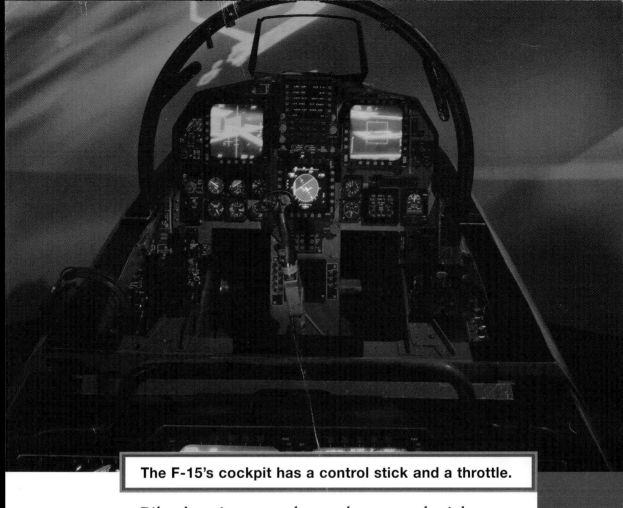

The F-15's cockpit has a control stick and a throttle.

Pilots' main controls are the control stick and the throttle. Pilots use the control stick to steer their planes. Machine gun controls also are on the control stick. Pilots control the speed of their aircraft with the throttle. Pilots also can use controls on the throttle to release missiles.

All F-15s have a screen called a head-up display (HUD). The HUD allows pilots to view flight information without looking down at cockpit controls.

F-15E Specifications

Function:	Air-to-ground attack aircraft
Manufacturer:	Boeing
Date Deployed:	1988
Length:	63 feet, 8 inches (19.4 meters)
Wingspan:	42 feet, 8 inches (13 meters)
Height:	18 feet, 5 inches (5.6 meters)
Weight:	81,000 pounds (36,700 kilograms)
Payload:	24,000 pounds (10,886 kilograms)
Engine:	Two Pratt & Whitney F100-PW-220 or 229 turbofans
Speed:	1,875 miles (3,017 kilometers) per hour
Range:	2,400 miles (3,862 kilometers); unlimited with in-flight refueling

F-15E LANTIRN System

The F-15E has a LANTIRN (Low Altitude Navigation Targeting Infrared for Night) system to help pilots perform missions at night and during bad weather conditions. The LANTIRN system is located under the aircraft's body in two storage areas called pods. One pod contains navigational equipment. This equipment helps the F-15E's crew keep track of the plane's surroundings. It includes a terrain-following radar (TFR)

F-15C/D Specifications

Function:	Tactical fighter
Manufacturer:	McDonnell Douglas/Boeing
Date Deployed:	1974
Length:	63 feet, 8 inches (19.4 meters)
Wingspan:	42 feet, 8 inches (13 meters)
Height:	18 feet, 5 inches (5.6 meters)
Weight:	68,000 pounds (30,844 kilograms)
Payload:	23,600 pounds (10,705 kilograms)
Engine:	Two Pratt & Whitney F100-PW-220 or 229 turbofans
Speed:	1,875 miles (3,017 kilometers) per hour
Range:	3,450 miles (5,552 kilometers); unlimited with in-flight refueling

and a forward-looking infrared (FLIR) sensor. The TFR allows pilots to see objects in their flight path on a screen. The FLIR sensor detects heat given off by objects. Information from the FLIR sensor appears on the pilot's HUD.

The second pod contains devices to help the F-15E's crew hit targets. A tracking FLIR sensor allows the crew to see targets on a screen. It can show targets that are up to 10 miles (16 kilometers) away.

nose

fuel tank

The F-15 Eagle

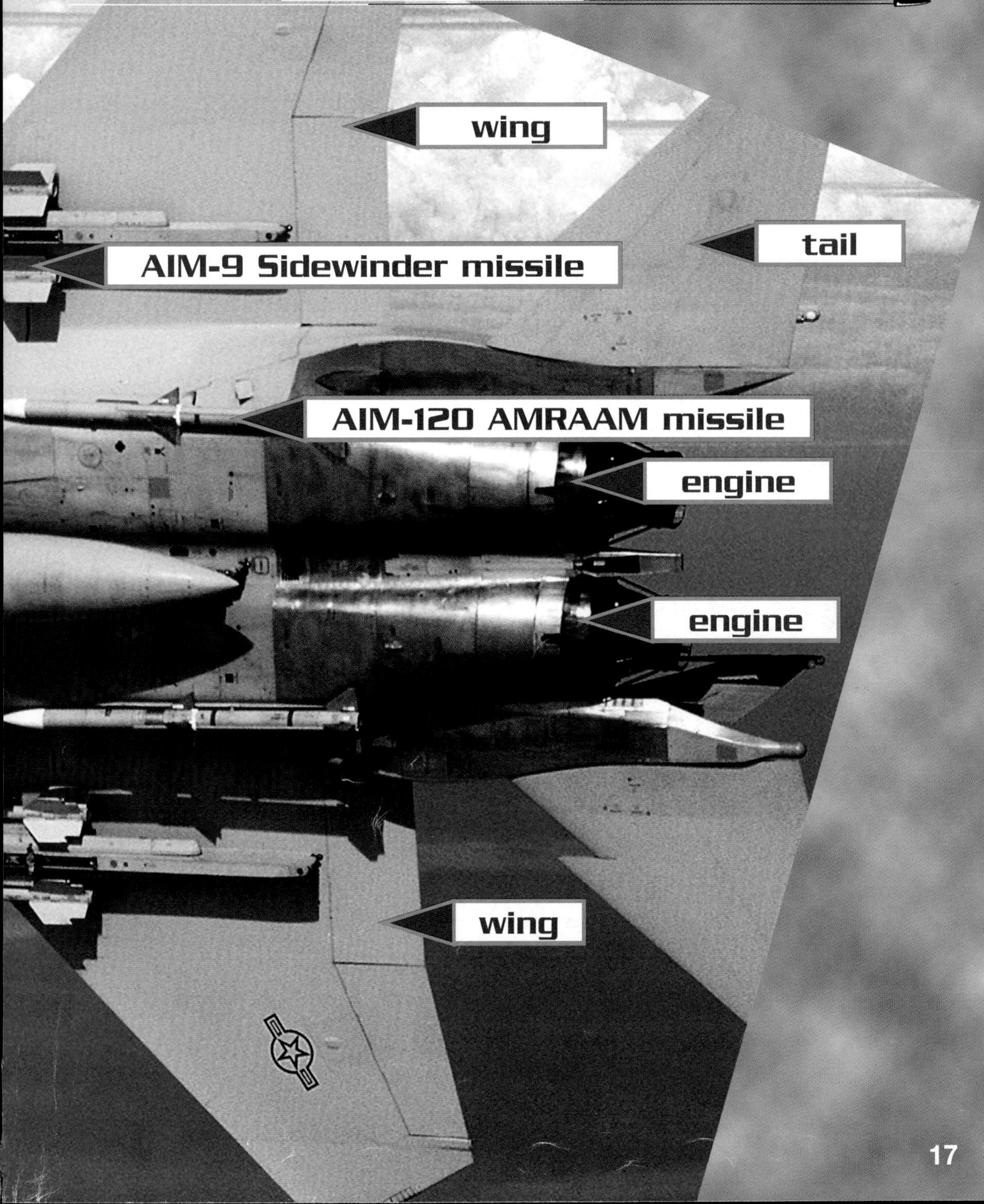

wing

tail

AIM-9 Sidewinder missile

AIM-120 AMRAAM missile

engine

engine

wing

Chapter Three

Learn About

- F-15 missiles
- Laser-guided bombs
- Protection systems

Weapons and Tactics

F-15s can carry equipment and weapons that weigh nearly 24,000 pounds (10,886 kilograms). All models can carry a large machine gun called a cannon and eight air-to-air missiles.

The F-15E usually carries bombs and air-to-ground missiles instead of air-to-air missiles. The F-15E has a Weapon System Operator (WSO). This crew member releases the F-15E's ground attack weapons and runs the plane's radar unit and protection systems.

The F-15 often carries the AIM-9 Sidewinder.

Automatic Cannon

The F-15's cannon is located in its right wing.
It is called the M-61A1 Vulcan cannon.

The M-61A1 holds bullets called rounds.
The cannon can fire more than 6,000 rounds
in one minute. It has a range of about .5 mile
(.8 kilometer).

Air-to-Air Missiles

The F-15 carries air-to-air missiles under its body and wings. The missiles can be heat-seeking or radar-guided missiles.

A heat-seeking missile has a sensor in its nose. The sensor guides the missile toward the heat from an enemy plane's exhaust. The F-15's heat-seeking missile is called the AIM-9 Sidewinder. It has a range of about 10 miles (16 kilometers).

F-15 pilots aim a radar beam at a target to fire radar-guided missiles. The missiles then follow the beam to the target. F-15 pilots often use the AIM-7 Sparrow missile at night and during bad weather conditions. The AIM-7 has a 90-pound (41-kilogram) explosive called a warhead in its nose. It has a range of about 30 miles (48 kilometers).

F-15 pilots use the radar-guided AIM-120 Advanced Medium Range Air-to-Air Missile (AMRAAM) for long-range targets. This missile has a range of almost 40 miles (64 kilometers).

F-15E Bombs

The F-15E can carry almost any of the Air Force's air-to-ground weapons. These weapons include unguided bombs and laser-guided bombs (LGBs). Unguided bombs fall to the ground freely. Laser beams guide LGBs to targets. An F-15E's WSO or a crew member from another plane aims a laser beam at a target. The LGB has a sensor that detects the beam of light.

The GBU-28 is one of the most powerful LGBs that the F-15E carries. The Air Force calls the GBU-28 the "Bunker Buster." It is designed to blow up underground enemy hideouts called bunkers. The GBU-28 weighs about 5,000 pounds (2,300 kilograms) and is almost 20 feet (6 meters) long.

F-15E Missiles

The F-15E sometimes carries air-to-ground missiles. The AGM-65G Maverick has a 300-pound (136-kilogram) warhead.

F-15Es sometimes carry Mark 84 LGBs.

It can hit targets more than 10 miles (16 kilometers) away.

WSOs can use the AGM-130 air-to-ground missile to hit long-range targets. The AGM-130 has a range of 40 miles (64 kilometers) and has a 2,000-pound (907-kilogram) warhead.

The F-15's low wing loading helps pilots turn easily.

Combat Tactics

The F-15 has features that help pilots control it during combat. It has low wing loading. The aircraft's weight is low compared to the size of its wings. The F-15 also has a great deal of thrust compared to its weight. These features help pilots make sharp turns at high speeds.

F-15 pilots need to know when enemy weapons approach their aircraft. The F-15 has a radar warning system. The system detects radar signals and shows their most likely source. Pilots can see this information on a cockpit screen.

The F-15E's WSO can try to protect the plane after receiving information from the radar warning system. The WSO may release small pieces of metal foil called chaff. Each metal strip reflects radar energy to the enemy radar station. The enemy radar then does not work properly. The WSO also can use the F-15E's radar jammer. The jammer sends out powerful electronic signals that stop enemy radar from working properly.

Chapter Four

Learn About

- F-15 improvements
- The F-22A Raptor
- Future of Air Force fighters

The Future

The F-15 has been one of the Air Force's most important fighters for more than 25 years. Throughout the years, the Air Force has updated much of the aircraft's equipment. Improvements make the plane's systems and weapons even more useful.

JDAMS

In 2003, the F-15E will carry a new type of smart bomb called the Joint Direct Attack Munition (JDAM). The JDAM includes a kit that fits over the tail of an unguided bomb to turn it into a guided bomb.

Spacecraft called satellites guide JDAMs. Poor weather conditions can cause LGBs to stray from their flight path. Weather conditions do not affect satellite-guided weapons.

The F-22A Raptor

Even with improvements, older F-15 models are wearing out. In the 1970s, the Air Force began planning to replace the F-15C. After testing experimental models, the Air Force chose the F-22A Raptor as the replacement plane. A two-seat version of the F-22A called the F-22B will replace the F-15D. The F-15E will remain in Air Force service until about 2030.

The F-22A will be the world's most advanced fighter plane. Each engine will produce about 35,000 pounds (16,000 kilograms) of thrust. It will use less fuel at high speeds than the F-15 does. Pilots of the F-22A will be able to fly

The F-22A will replace the F-15C in the future.

1,500 miles (2,400 kilometers) per hour for long periods of time.

Lockheed Martin and Boeing produce the F-22A. In the late 1990s, the Air Force flew test models of the fighter. Air Force officials hope to put F-22s into service in the early 2000s.

Words to Know

canopy (KAN-uh-pee)—a cover over an airplane cockpit

chaff (CHAF)—strips of metal foil dropped by an aircraft to confuse enemy radar

exhaust (eg-ZAWST)—heated air leaving a jet engine

laser beam (LAY-zur BEEM)—a narrow, intense beam of light

radar (RAY-dar)—equipment that uses radio waves to locate and guide objects

sensor (SEN-sur)—an instrument that detects physical changes in the environment

throttle (THROT-uhl)—a control on an airplane that allows pilots to increase or decrease the plane's speed

thrust (THRUHST)—the force created by a jet engine; thrust pushes an airplane forward.

warhead (WOR-hed)—the explosive part of a missile or rocket

To Learn More

Graham, Ian. *Attack Fighters.* Designed for Success. New York: Heinemann, 2003.

Holden, Henry M. *Air Force Aircraft.* Aircraft. Berkeley Heights, N.J.: Enslow, 2001.

Loves, June. *Military Aircraft.* Flight. Philadelphia: Chelsea House, 2001.

Useful Addresses

Air Combat Command
Office of Public Affairs
115 Thompson Street, Suite 211
Langley AFB, VA 23665

United States Air Force Museum
110 Spaatz Street
Wright-Patterson AFB, OH 45433

Internet Sites

Track down many sites about F-15 Eagles.
Visit the FACT HOUND at *http://www.facthound.com*

IT IS EASY! IT IS FUN!

1) Go to *http://www.facthound.com*
2) Type in: 0736815112
3) Click on "FETCH IT" and FACT HOUND will find
   several links hand-picked by our editors.

Relax and let our pal FACT HOUND do the research for you!

Index

A Buddy Book by Sarah Tieck

GET HEALTHY

Be Safe

ABDO Publishing Company

VISIT US AT
www.abdopublishing.com

Published by ABDO Publishing Company, PO Box 398166, Minneapolis, MN 55439.

Copyright © 2012 by Abdo Consulting Group, Inc. International copyrights reserved in all countries. No part of this book may be reproduced in any form without written permission from the publisher. Buddy Books™ is a trademark and logo of ABDO Publishing Company.

Printed in the United States of America, North Mankato, Minnesota.
102011
012012

 PRINTED ON RECYCLED PAPER

Coordinating Series Editor: Rochelle Baltzer
Contributing Editors: Megan M. Gunderson, BreAnn Rumsch, Marcia Zappa
Graphic Design: Jenny Christensen
Cover Photograph: *Shutterstock*: AISPIX.
Interior Photographs/Illustrations: *AP Photo*: Journal Times, Scott Anderson (p. 23), Damian Dovarganes (p. 27); *Eighth Street Studio* (p. 26); *iStockphoto*: ©iStockphoto.com/CEFutcher (p. 13), ©iStockphoto.com/DanielBendjy (p. 25), ©iStockphoto.com/JayLazarin (p. 17), ©iStockphoto.com/kali9 (pp. 7, 30), ©iStockphoto.com/LeggNet (p. 29), ©iStockphoto.com/lisafx (p. 23), ©iStockphoto.com/monkeybusinessimages (pp. 9, 11), ©iStockphoto.com/spxChrome (p. 19); *Photo Researchers, Inc.*: Jim Dowdalls (p. 21); *Shutterstock*: Galina Barskaya (p. 30), sonya etchison (pp. 5, 19), MANDY GODBEHEAR (p. 13), Kzenon (p. 26), Maridav (p. 25), Layland Masuda (p. 15), Morgan Lane Photography (p. 5), Orange Line Media (p. 5).

Library of Congress Cataloging-in-Publication Data

Tieck, Sarah, 1976-
  Be safe / Sarah Tieck.
    p. cm. -- (Get healthy)
  ISBN 978-1-61783-231-4
  1. Safety education--Juvenile literature. I. Title.
  HV675.5.T545 2012
  613.6--dc23
                    2011034602

Table of Contents

Healthy Living

Your body is amazing! It does thousands of things each day. It lets you jump, learn, and hear. A healthy body helps you feel good and live well!

In order to be healthy, you must take care of your body. One way to do this is to be safe. So, let's learn more about how you can protect yourself!

Safety is important when playing outside, riding in a car, and surfing the Internet.

Danger Danger

The world is a cool and fun place! But, there is also danger. Every day, people get hurt in accidents, crimes, or disasters.

Some people worry bad things could happen. But, worrying doesn't keep you or other people safe. The best way to stay safe is to learn how to protect yourself. Then, you'll make smart choices.

Sometimes worry turns into anxiety. Anxiety can be hard on your body. It can make your muscles tight and your heart beat fast. It can also cause breathing trouble.

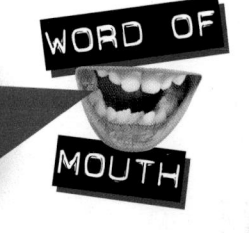

WORD OF MOUTH

Other people can help you feel better. Share your worries with someone you trust.

Home Sweet Home

Most people feel very safe at home. But, places that feel safe can be unsafe. So, it is important to be aware.

In the kitchen, have an adult help you use the stove, oven, or blender. And, wash your hands before and after handling raw meat or eggs.

Some people keep guns in their homes. If you see a gun, do not touch it. Tell an adult right way. He or she will move the gun to a safe spot.

Stranger Danger

Stranger safety is important. At home, keep doors and windows locked. Don't tell strangers if you are home alone. Don't open the door to them. And, never let them into your house.

In public, you can't tell which strangers are nice and which are not. Protect yourself by staying in well-lit, open places with lots of people. And, always tell an adult where you are going.

At a store, stay close to people you know. Avoid walking off alone.

WORD OF MOUTH

If a stranger talks to you, it is okay to walk away. If you think you are in danger, yell loudly and run away.

Safe at School

Most of the time, your school is a safe place. But sometimes, kids hit, kick, or push other kids. They may tease or **threaten** them. This is called bullying. If you feel unsafe at school, talk to an adult. He or she can help.

Kids may also try to **pressure** each other to act in a certain way. You never have to do something you don't think is right. Just say no!

Bullies can hurt your body and your feelings.

On the Web

Even though you may be at home or school, the Internet is a public place. Other people online are strangers. So, don't chat with people you don't know.

Follow the Internet safety rules your family and teachers set. Remember, never share personal information online. This includes your name, phone number, and address.

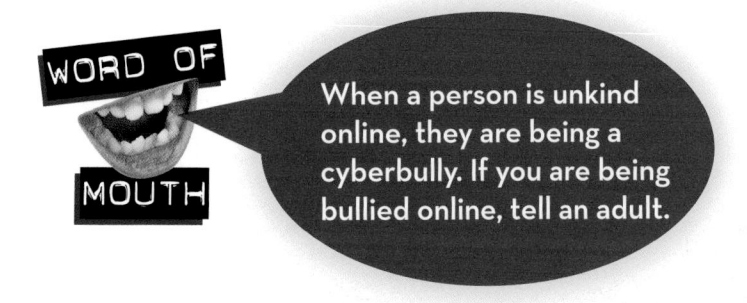

WORD OF MOUTH

When a person is unkind online, they are being a cyberbully. If you are being bullied online, tell an adult.

Ask an adult which Web sites are safe to visit.

Crime Watch

Do you ever watch police shows on television? Well, crime also happens in real life. Some people break into houses, stores, or cars to steal things. Others use drugs or join gangs.

Crimes are scary. But by being aware, you can help **protect** yourself from harm. Trust your feelings. If something makes you feel unsafe, leave right away. Then, tell an adult or call the police.

WORD OF MOUTH

If you go into a public bathroom by yourself, let your parent or guardian know. And, be aware of other people in the bathroom.

Police officers can help you if you are in trouble.

Help Is on the Way!

If you are in serious danger, calling 9-1-1 is a way to get help. Call if there is an accident or an emergency. You can also call to report a crime. Dialing 9-1-1 tells police officers, firefighters, and the hospital that you are in trouble.

If you call 9-1-1, explain your emergency and where you are. Help will come very quickly. So, only call this number if you really need it. And, don't hang up until you are told it's okay to.

When someone calls 9-1-1, firefighters may be the first to arrive to help.

Sometimes, buildings catch fire. Most have fire alarms to let you know there is a fire. If you hear an alarm beep, leave fast. Then call 9-1-1.

WORD OF MOUTH

In a car, tell the driver if you see or hear an ambulance, police car, or fire truck. When drivers slow down to stop or let them pass, they help save lives.

Watch Out

When you are in danger, you will often feel afraid. You might get goosebumps on your arms and legs. Other times, you might just have a funny feeling.

When there is danger, parts of your brain act quickly to protect you. This is known as the fight-or-flight response. It allows you to think and move quickly to avoid danger.

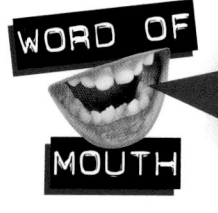

WORD OF MOUTH

You might feel afraid even when you are safe! Sometimes, scary thoughts or feelings can cause your body to act. If you feel afraid, try to stay calm and talk to an adult.

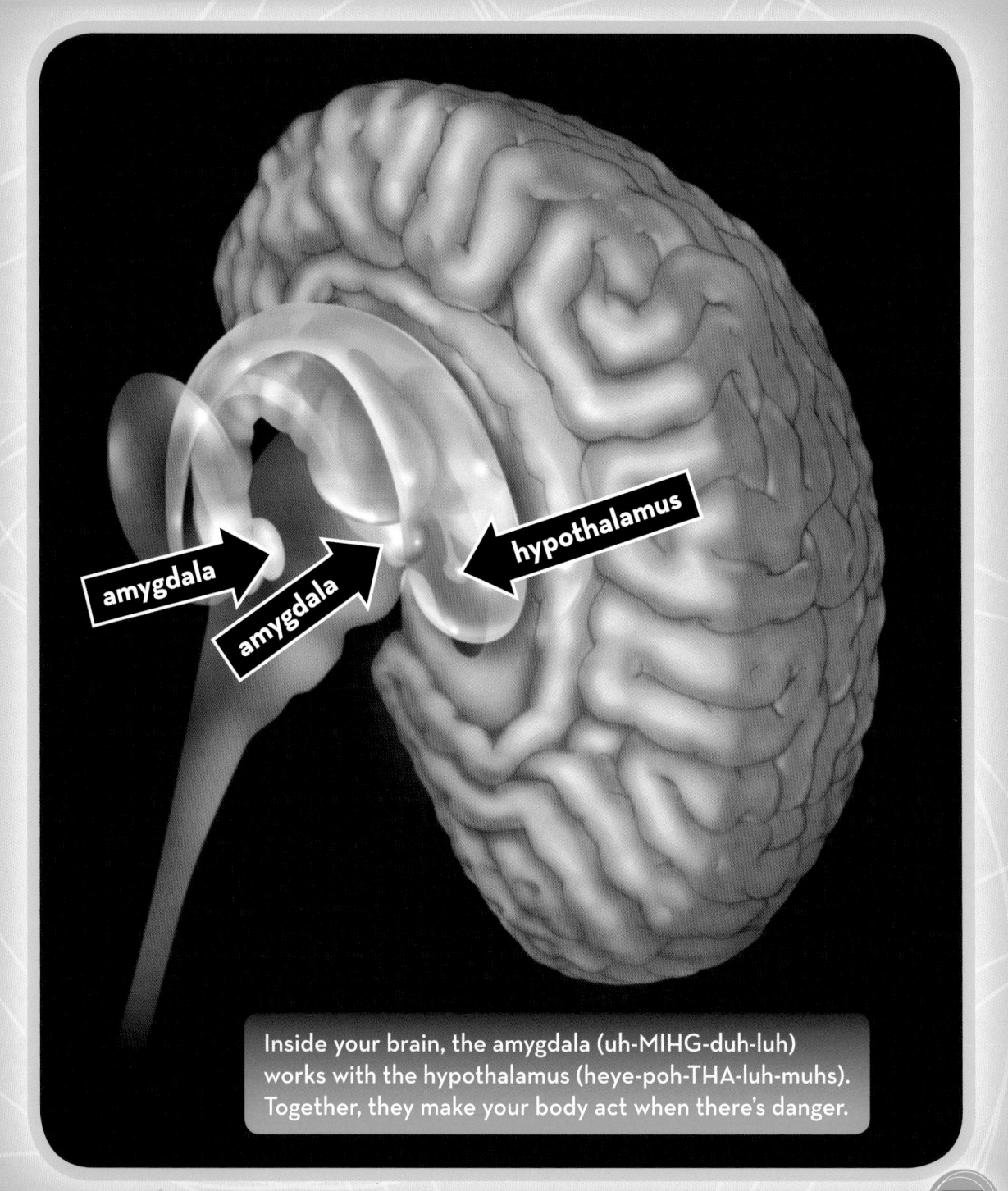

amygdala

amygdala

hypothalamus

Inside your brain, the amygdala (uh-MIHG-duh-luh) works with the hypothalamus (heye-poh-THA-luh-muhs). Together, they make your body act when there's danger.

Now and Later

Learning is a major part of staying safe. It is a good idea to learn first aid. This includes knowing how to clean cuts and apply bandages.

To protect yourself from disasters, learn about the area where you live. Talk to your family about what to do in an emergency. That way, you will know how to act if you are ever in a disaster.

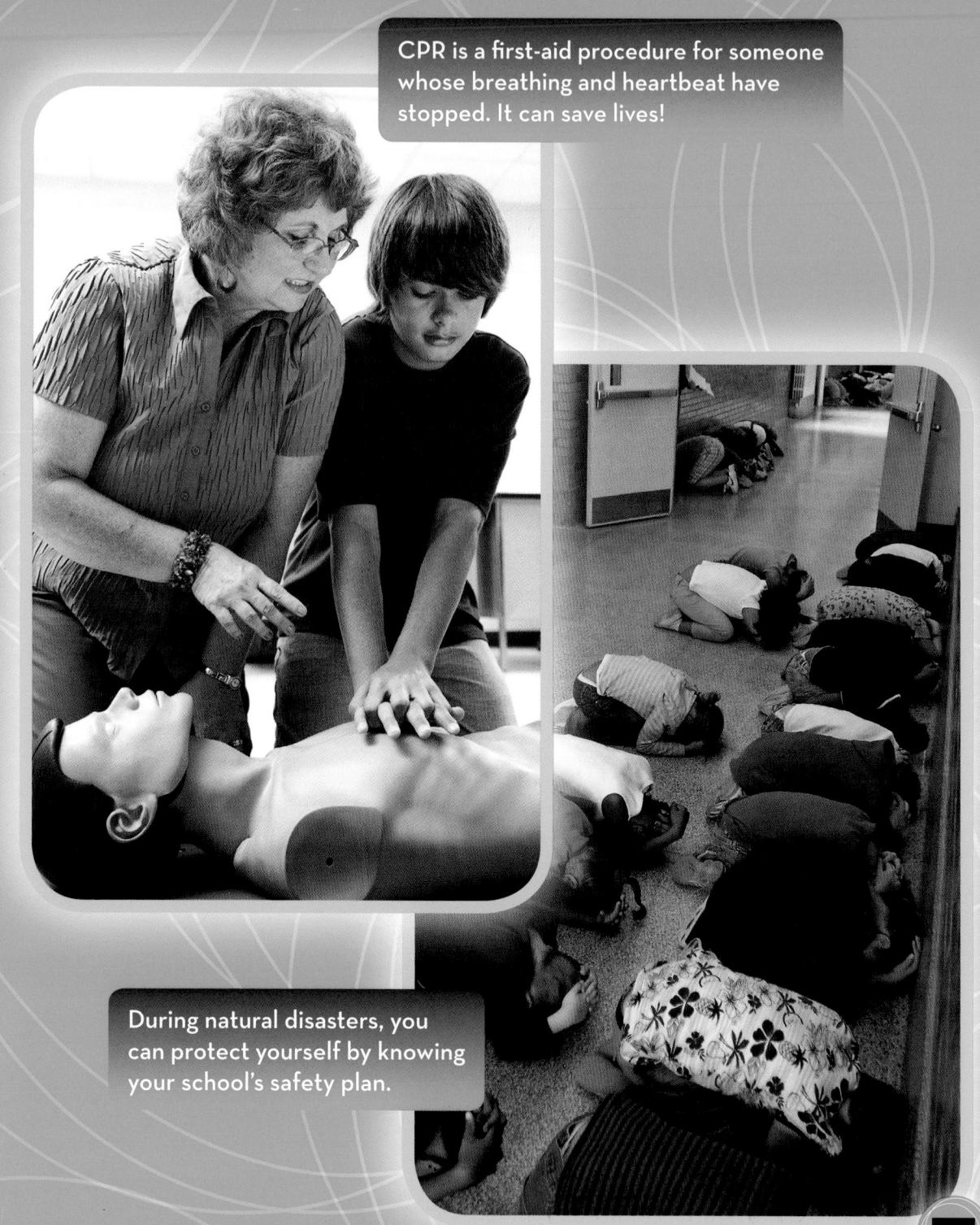

CPR is a first-aid procedure for someone whose breathing and heartbeat have stopped. It can save lives!

During natural disasters, you can protect yourself by knowing your school's safety plan.

23

It is important to live in a safe and careful way. If you put yourself in danger, you may be hurt. So, take safety seriously. Make good choices now, and take care of yourself for many years!

Keep fun activities safe! Wear helmets and life jackets to protect yourself.

Brain Food

What should I do if I get lost in a public place?

Stay in a public place. Look for an adult to help you. At a store, someone who works there may be safe to ask. You can also look for police officers, security guards, or women with children.

What if there is an emergency at my school?

Listen carefully for directions from your teacher or another adult. Schools often practice how to act during emergencies. So, pay attention during practice drills!

What if someone tries to kidnap me?

If anyone tries to hurt or kidnap you, it is important to get away. Scream loudly so others can hear. And, run away. When you get to a safe place, ask an adult for help.

Making Healthy Choices

Remember that being safe keeps you alive and healthy! Learn safety skills. Pay attention to what is happening around you and how you feel. Then, you can better **protect** yourself from danger.

Safety is just one part of a healthy life. Each positive choice you make will keep you healthy!

WORD OF MOUTH

Try not to worry about things that are unlikely to happen. That makes it harder for you to notice real danger.

Look both ways before
crossing the street

BODY TALK

✔ If you feel scared, your muscles may get tight. This is meant to help you run or fight against danger!

✔ Your heart beats faster when you are scared. This gets your body ready to move.

ON THE GO

✔ Helmets and pads keep you safe when you are skateboarding.

JOIN IN

✔ Get to know your neighbors! Together, you can take part in neighborhood safety programs such as National Night Out.

Important Words

accident an unplanned event that may result in harm or injury.

disaster (dih-ZAS-tuhr) an event that causes damage and suffering.

emergency (ih-MUHR-juhnt-see) an unexpected event that requires immediate action.

first aid emergency treatment given to a sick or hurt person.

pressure (PREH-shuhr) the force you feel when people try to get you to do something.

protect (pruh-TEHKT) to guard against harm or danger.

threaten to say that you will harm someone or something.

Web Sites

To learn more about being safe, visit ABDO Publishing Company online. Web sites about being safe are featured on our Book Links page. These links are routinely monitored and updated to provide the most current information available.

www.abdopublishing.com

Index

311920203747789